Fact Finders®

THE
INVENTION
OF THE
AEROPLANE

Lucy Beevor

raintree
a Capstone company — publishers for children

Raintree is an imprint of Capstone Global Library Limited, a company incorporated in England and Wales having its registered office at 264 Banbury Road, Oxford, OX2 7DY – Registered company number: 66955

www.raintree.co.uk
myorders@raintree.co.uk

Text © Capstone Global Library Limited 2018
The moral rights of the proprietor have been asserted.

Edited by Jennifer Huston
Designed by Heidi Thompson
Original illustrations © Capstone Global Library Ltd 2018
Picture research by Eric Gohl
Production by Katy LaVigne
Originated by Capstone Global Library Ltd
Printed and bound in Inida.

Original Edition Author
Julie L. Sinclair

ISBN 978 1 4747 5282 4
22 21 20 19 18
10 9 8 7 6 5 4 3 2 1

British Library Cataloguing in Publication Data
A full catalogue record for this book is available from the British Library.

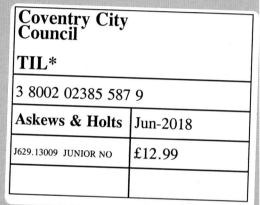

Acknowledgements
We would like to thank the following for permission to reproduce photographs:
Alamy: ClassicStock, 7, Niday Picture Library, 6; Getty Images: Underwood Archives, 21; Granger, NYC: 12; Library of Congress: 15; Newscom: akg-images, 13, Everett Collection, 20, Picture History, 4 (all), UIG Universal Images Group/Underwood Archives, 23; Shutterstock: Carlos E. Santa Maria, 24, Chris Parypa Photography, 26, Ensuper, cover (middle), Everett Historical, 8, 9, fotoslaz, cover (top left & bottom), goodmoments, 17, Graham Bloomfield, 25, ifong, 2–3, 18–19, Michal Jurkowski, cover (top right), Nicku, 11, phive, cover (middle left), vectorEps, 22, Wojciech Beczynski, cover (middle right); Thinkstock: Claudio Divizia, 10;
Design Elements: Shutterstock

Every effort has been made to contact copyright holders of material reproduced in this book. Any omissions will be rectified in subsequent printings if notice is given to the publisher.

All the internet addresses (URLs) given in this book were valid at the time of going to press. However, due to the dynamic nature of the internet, some addresses may have changed, or sites may have changed or ceased to exist since publication.
While the author and publisher regret any inconvenience this may cause readers, no responsibility for any such changes can be accepted by either the author or the publisher.

CONTENTS

1 ▶ A GIFT FOR TWO BOYS

One day in 1878, Milton Wright brought a gift home for his two youngest sons. Orville was 7 years old. Wilbur was 11. The gift was a toy helicopter made out of cork, bamboo, paper and a rubber band.

Orville (left) and Wilbur Wright grew up in the United States in the late 1800s. They dreamed of one day building and flying an aeroplane.

Milton showed the boys how to make the helicopter fly. He wound the two **propellers** and threw the toy into the air. The boys were amazed when the helicopter flew. Eventually the helicopter broke, but it had sparked their imaginations. From that day forward, Wilbur and Orville wanted to build a flying machine. One day they hoped to travel in the machine and fly through the sky.

DID YOU KNOW?

Children played with toy helicopters for more than 100 years before full-sized aircraft were built.

propeller rotating blade that provides the force to move an aircraft through the air
aircraft vehicle that flies through the air

BEFORE THE AEROPLANE

2

Until the late 1800s, most people did not travel very far from their homes. They travelled by horse and cart or they walked. For those who needed to travel long distances, it took weeks – sometimes months – to get to their **destinations**. But scientists and inventors were building new machines that would change travel forever.

Travelling by horse and cart was slow and uncomfortable.

destination place to which someone is travelling

NEW WAYS TO TRAVEL

Engines powered by steam, petrol and electricity led to the invention of trains and cars, which could travel longer distances. They were much faster than walking or travelling by horse. This made it easier for people to travel farther away from home.

The invention of the steam train allowed people to travel longer distances more quickly.

DID YOU KNOW?

The UK's railway system is the oldest in the world. The Swansea and Mumbles Railway in Wales carried the world's first fare-paying passengers on 25 March 1807.

Trains and cars did not fix all travel problems. Cars didn't always make travelling easy. Early cars were uncomfortable. They did not have springs to make the ride smooth. They also didn't have heaters. Early cars were unsafe and difficult to drive. Plus, there were very few road rules, which often led to accidents.

Early cars were not easy to drive and that sometimes led to accidents.

Trains had problems too. They could only travel where there were railway tracks, so they didn't go everywhere people wanted to go. Trains also needed many workers to maintain the tracks. A train could run off its tracks if the tracks were damaged.

Trains were not always a safe way to travel. The Great Chatsworth Train Wreck occurred in Illinois, USA, in 1887. More than 80 people were killed.

People wanted to make travelling easier and safer. Some inventors made better engines for cars, but others began to think about a new way of travelling. They dreamed of flying through the air like birds.

GREAT INVENTORS

3

Before and after the inventions of the train and car, people tried to work out how to build machines that would carry them safely through the air.

LEONARDO DA VINCI

Leonardo da Vinci was one of the first people to **design** a flying machine. Da Vinci lived in Italy in the late 1400s and early 1500s. He designed several machines with flapping wings that he called "ornithopters".

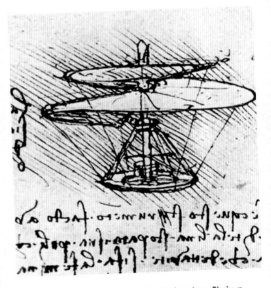

Leonardo da Vinci sketched a flying machine he called an airscrew. It is similar to a modern-day helicopter.

DID YOU KNOW?

Leonardo da Vinci designed many early machines. They included an armoured car, a parachute and another type of flying machine that looked like a helicopter.

THE MONTGOLFIER BROTHERS

In 1783, Joseph-Michel and Jacques-Étienne Montgolfier built a hot-air balloon. But the French brothers were not sure if it was safe for passengers. To find out, they put a sheep, a duck and a chicken in the balloon's basket. These animals became the world's first hot-air balloon passengers. The animals landed safely after being in the air for about eight minutes. In November of that year, the first human passengers took a 25-minute flight over Paris in the Montgolfier brothers' balloon.

The Montgolfier brothers tested their first hot-air balloon in 1783.

design create the shape or style of something

SIR GEORGE CAYLEY

In 1804, British **engineer** Sir George Cayley built a special model **glider**. With a movable tail and a kite-shaped set of wings on a stick, it looked somewhat like a modern aeroplane. By 1853, Cayley had created the first full-sized glider. When he asked his assistant to fly the glider, the test was a success. It was the first glider flight to carry a passenger.

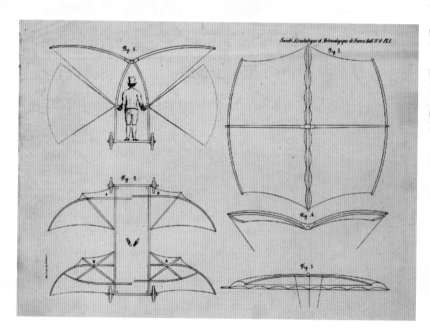

Sir George Cayley is sometimes called the father of **aviation**. This illustration shows his drawing of the glider.

engineer someone trained to design and build machines, vehicles, bridges, roads or other structures
glider lightweight aircraft that flies by floating and rising on air currents instead of by engine power
aviation science of building and flying aircraft

OTTO LILIENTHAL

German inventor Otto Lilienthal built his first flying machine in 1891. This hang-glider had large wings and could soar through the air. Lilienthal later built many other successful gliders.

Otto Lilienthal made more than 2,000 flights in his hang-gliders. Some of them reached more than 305 metres (1,000 feet) up in the air.

THE WRIGHT BROTHERS

Wilbur and Orville Wright studied flying and **mechanics** for many years. They tested models and built and flew large gliders and kites. But they wanted to build a flying machine that powered itself.

The brothers worked hard to make an aeroplane. They designed and built a lightweight engine and also made a propeller. Finally, in December 1903, their first aeroplane was ready. They called it the *Flyer*. It measured 6.4 metres (21 feet) long and its wings were 12.3 metres (40.5 feet) wide. It weighed 274.4 kilograms (605 pounds) without a pilot.

mechanics part of science that deals with the way forces affect still or moving objects

TAKING TO THE SKIES

On 17 December 1903, the brothers took the *Flyer* to the sand dunes near Kitty Hawk, North Carolina. Orville sat in the pilot's seat, and Wilbur ran alongside. Their plane flew 37 metres (120 feet) in 12 seconds. It was the first time that a self-powered machine had risen, flown in a straight line and landed safely.

The Wright brothers flew the *Flyer* for the first time on 17 December 1903. It was only in the air for 12 seconds, but it made history.

4 HOW AEROPLANES WORK

The four forces of flight help to explain how aeroplanes fly. These forces are **thrust**, **lift**, weight and **drag**.

THRUST AND LIFT

Thrust moves an aeroplane forward. A jet engine creates thrust and pushes the aeroplane forward. Most propeller engines also pull the plane forward. Thrust works with lift to make the aeroplane rise and fly.

Lift allows an aeroplane to rise off the ground. An aeroplane's wings are designed to create lift when the plane is moving. Lift happens when air moves faster on top of a wing than below it. This movement of air takes pressure off of the top of a wing. Lift allows the plane to rise.

WEIGHT AND DRAG

Weight is the force of **gravity**. Gravity pulls objects down to Earth. An aeroplane has to fight weight (gravity) to stay in the air. Weight would make an aeroplane fall towards Earth if the engine did not produce enough thrust to keep it moving forward.

Drag also works against the aeroplane. Drag is the force of **friction**. Friction slows objects down when they move against each other. Wind is a type of drag because it slows down the plane as it moves over the aircraft.

The forces of flight help make even the simplest aeroplanes fly.

thrust force that pushes a vehicle forward
lift upward force of air that causes an object to fly
drag force that resists the motion of an object moving through the air
gravity force that pulls objects with mass together; gravity pulls objects down towards the centre of Earth
friction force created when two objects rub together; friction slows down objects

THE FOUR FORCES OF FLIGHT

The Wright brothers could build and fly an aeroplane because they understood the four forces of flight needed to make a plane fly.

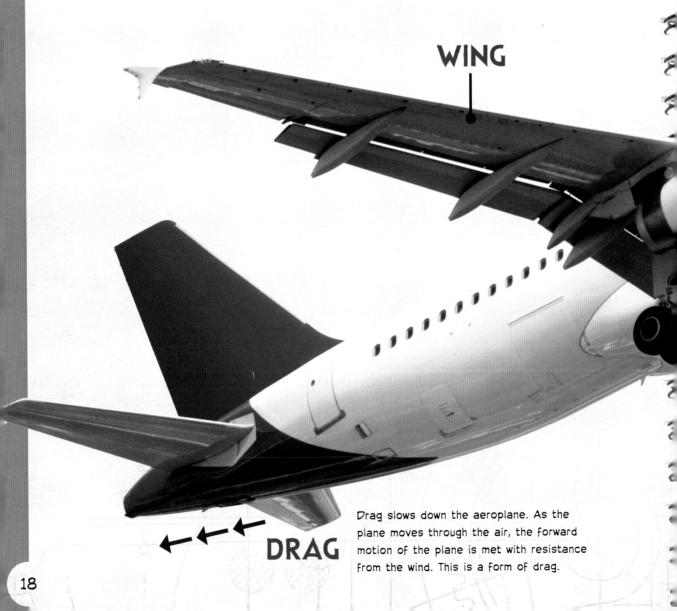

WING

DRAG

Drag slows down the aeroplane. As the plane moves through the air, the forward motion of the plane is met with resistance from the wind. This is a form of drag.

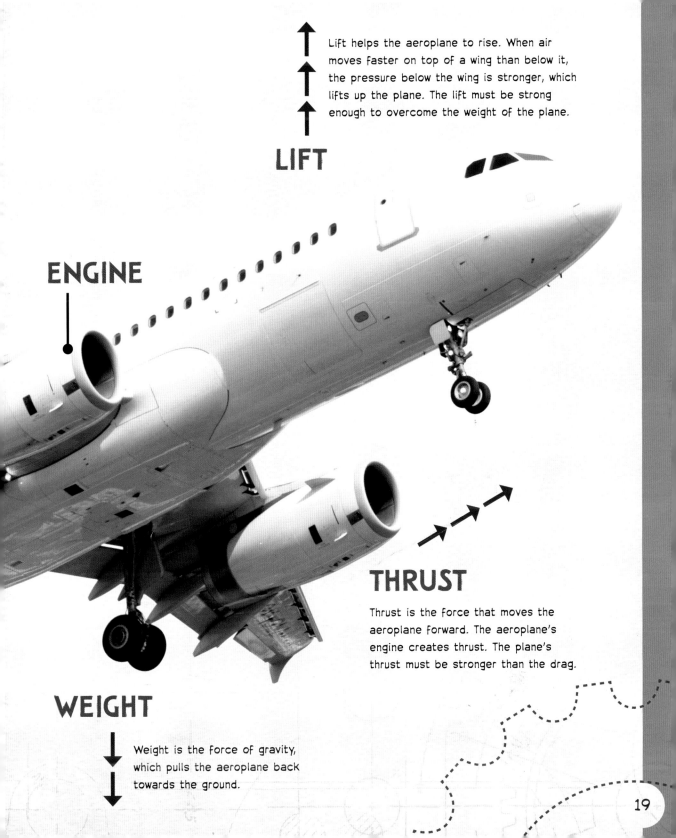

LIFT

Lift helps the aeroplane to rise. When air moves faster on top of a wing than below it, the pressure below the wing is stronger, which lifts up the plane. The lift must be strong enough to overcome the weight of the plane.

ENGINE

THRUST

Thrust is the force that moves the aeroplane forward. The aeroplane's engine creates thrust. The plane's thrust must be stronger than the drag.

WEIGHT

Weight is the force of gravity, which pulls the aeroplane back towards the ground.

19

5 THE WORLD BEGINS TO FLY

Aeroplanes changed the world. It wasn't long before many countries realized that aeroplanes could be useful. In 1908, the Wright brothers began making planes for the US Army. Aeroplanes were first used to carry weapons during World War I (1914–1918). During World War II (1939–1945), aeroplanes were one of the main vehicles used in battle.

World War I was the first war in which aeroplanes were widely used.

WARPLANES

At first, warplane pilots simply flew over enemy territory to spy on them. The pilots wanted to get information on the enemy's location and number of troops and weapons. They used this information to prepare the ground troops for battle. Next, warplanes added machine guns and fierce fighting took place in the skies. Later, a special hatch was added to warplanes so they could drop bombs over enemy territory. It wasn't until World War II that planes were used to transport troops.

The aeroplane also changed travel and business. The first passenger plane began service in Florida, USA, in 1914. The plane took off and landed on water and carried one passenger at a time. For £3.80 (about £413 today), a person could cross Tampa Bay in about 20 minutes. A boat took 2 hours to make the same trip. A train took 4 to 12 hours because it had to go all the way around the water. Going by car took 20 hours at the time.

Passengers board an aeroplane in the 1920s.

CHARLES LINDBERGH

In the early 1900s, many people were afraid to travel by aeroplane. They thought planes were unsafe.

But Charles Lindbergh changed the way people felt about flying. In 1927, he flew from New York City, USA, to Paris, France. He was the first person to fly alone across the Atlantic Ocean. His flight made people excited about air travel. After his flight, more businesses started building aeroplanes to carry passengers.

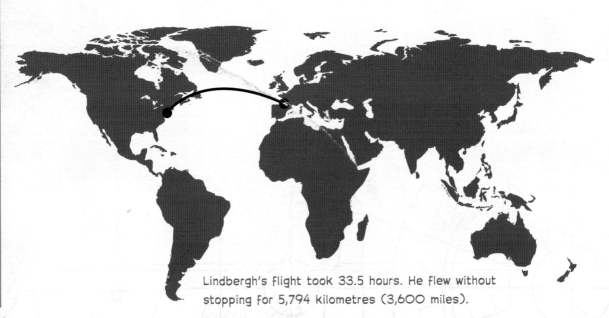

Lindbergh's flight took 33.5 hours. He flew without stopping for 5,794 kilometres (3,600 miles).

NEW LAWS

Laws were introduced to make aeroplanes safer for passengers. In the UK, the Air Navigation and Transport Act of 1920 made many rules for air travel. Planes had to be tested for safety, and pilots had to pass tests before they were allowed to fly.

In 1972, the Civil Aviation Authority (CAA) was formed in the UK. One of the CAA's jobs is to make sure aeroplanes fly safely.

Charles Lindbergh stands next to his aeroplane, the *Spirit of St. Louis*. In 1927, Lindbergh flew his plane across the Atlantic Ocean.

6 AEROPLANES TODAY

After the Wright brothers, inventors began making aeroplanes larger and faster. They also added controls to make planes safer. These instruments help pilots to fly at night or in bad weather. Radar and **air traffic control** also make flying safer.

Today's aeroplanes have lots of safety controls.

PASSENGER PLANES

The first modern passenger plane was the Boeing 247, which was introduced in 1933. The Boeing 247 travelled at a speed of 304 kilometres (189 miles) per hour and carried just 10 passengers.

In 1976, Concorde became the first aeroplane to make **supersonic** passenger flights. It could fly more than 2,092 kilometres (1,300 miles) per hour. In fact, it only took 3.5 hours to fly from London to New York City. Even today, it takes other planes 8 hours to make the same trip. However, only the very rich could afford to fly on Concorde. By 2003, when Concorde made its last flight, a one-way ticket from London to New York City cost more than £4,350.

DID YOU KNOW?

Because Concorde travelled so fast, it needed more fuel to fly it. On average, Concorde used about 25,627 litres (6,770 gallons) of fuel per hour. That's four times as much as an ordinary jet plane.

air traffic control ground staff who monitor and direct aeroplanes in flight and before and after take-off
supersonic faster than the speed of sound (1,234 kilometres/767 miles per hour)

Today, most passenger planes fly 740–925 kilometres (460–575 miles) per hour. But engineers continue to build faster aeroplanes. There are currently plans to build other supersonic planes, similar to Concorde, but with much more affordable ticket prices.

The F–15 Eagle is one of the most successful US military planes in combat history. It has a top speed of 3,018 kilometres (1,875 miles) per hour.

DID YOU KNOW?

Today, the largest passenger plane is the Airbus A380. It has two floors and can carry up to 615 passengers.

Some military planes can fly more than 2,897 kilometres (1,800 miles) per hour. In 2004, NASA set a world record with a **scramjet engine**-powered aircraft that reached nearly 11,265 kilometres (7,000 miles) per hour! That's almost 10 times faster than the speed of sound!

Over time, planes have become a fairly common way to travel. There are more than 100,000 flights all over the world every day. These flights carry hundreds of millions of passengers to their destinations.

Travelling by plane has also become much safer. Pilots train for years before they can fly an aeroplane. Plus, two pilots are required to fly passenger planes – a captain and a co-pilot. If something happens to the captain during a flight, the co-pilot can step in and land the plane safely.

INTO SPACE

The aeroplanes of the future could be faster and hold more passengers. They could even travel to space! The Virgin Galactic company is testing a passenger plane called WhiteKnightTwo that could be fast and powerful enough to one day take passengers into space and back.

scramjet engine type of engine in which combustion takes place in supersonic airflow

NOTABLE AEROPLANES SINCE 1914

THE ST. PETERSBURG–TAMPA AIRBOAT LINE
1914
1 pilot, 1 passenger
103 kilometres (64 miles) per hour

SPIRIT OF ST. LOUIS
1927
1 pilot
193 kilometres (120 miles) per hour

BOEING 247
1933
2 pilots, 10 passengers
304 kilometres (189 miles) per hour

CONCORDE
1976
2 pilots, 100 passengers
2,179 kilometres (1,354 miles) per hour

AIRBUS A380
2005
2 pilots, 544–615 passengers
945 kilometres (587 miles) per hour

TIMELINE

1480s	Leonardo da Vinci draws designs for his ornithopter
1783	The Montgolfier brothers test the first hot-air balloon
1804	Sir George Cayley builds a special model glider that looks somewhat like a modern aeroplane
1853	Cayley creates the first full-scale glider that makes a successful flight with a passenger
1891	Otto Lilienthal makes his first hang-glider and becomes the first person to make repeated successful flights
1903	Wilbur and Orville Wright build and launch the *Flyer*, the world's first successful aeroplane
1914	The first aircraft passenger service begins in Florida, USA
1914–1918	Many new military aeroplanes are created for use in World War I
1927	Charles Lindbergh becomes the first person to fly alone across the Atlantic Ocean
1933	The Boeing 247 becomes the first modern passenger plane
1976	Concorde becomes the first passenger plane to fly supersonic (faster than the speed of sound)
2003	Concorde is retired because of low passenger numbers
2005	The Airbus A380, the world's largest passenger plane, makes its first passenger flight

GLOSSARY

aircraft vehicle that flies through the air

air traffic control ground staff who monitor and direct aeroplanes in flight and before and after take-off

aviation science of building and flying aircraft

design create the shape or style of something

destination place to which someone is travelling

drag force that resists the motion of an object moving through the air

engineer someone trained to design and build machines, vehicles, bridges, roads or other structures

friction force created when two objects rub together; friction slows down objects

glider lightweight aircraft that flies by floating and rising on air currents instead of by engine power

gravity force that pulls objects with mass together; gravity pulls objects down towards the centre of Earth

lift upward force of air that causes an object to fly

mechanics part of science that deals with the way forces affect still or moving objects

propeller rotating blade that provides the force to move an aircraft through the air

scramjet engine type of engine in which combustion takes place in supersonic airflow

supersonic faster than the speed of sound (1,234 kilometres/767 miles per hour)

thrust force that pushes a vehicle forward

COMPREHENSION QUESTIONS

1. Until the late 1800s, most people did not travel very far from their homes. Travel was often slow and uncomfortable. In what ways have aeroplanes made travel better?

2. Choose two aeroplanes from the book, one early and one modern. Using the text and photos, compare and contrast the two aeroplanes. How has the modern plane changed from the early one?

3. Imagine you are one of the first passengers on Virgin Galactic's WhiteKnightTwo aircraft into space. Describe your experience on board the historic flight.

FIND OUT MORE

Cars, Trains, Ships & Planes: A Visual Encyclopedia of Every Vehicle, Clive Gifford (DK Publishing, 2015)

Great Aircraft Designs 1900 – Today (Iconic Designs), Richard Spilsbury (Raintree, 2016)

Planes and Helicopters: An Accidental History of Inventions (It'll Never Work), Jon Richards (Franklin Watts, 2016)

WEBSITES

kids.britannica.com/kids/article/airplane/352719

Check out this overview of the history of aeroplanes.

www.dkfindout.com/uk/transport/history-aircraft/
This article offers a brief history of aircraft, from balloons to gliders to jets.

www.sciencelearn.org.nz/resources/305-people-in-flight-history

Learn more about some of the pioneers of flight.

INDEX